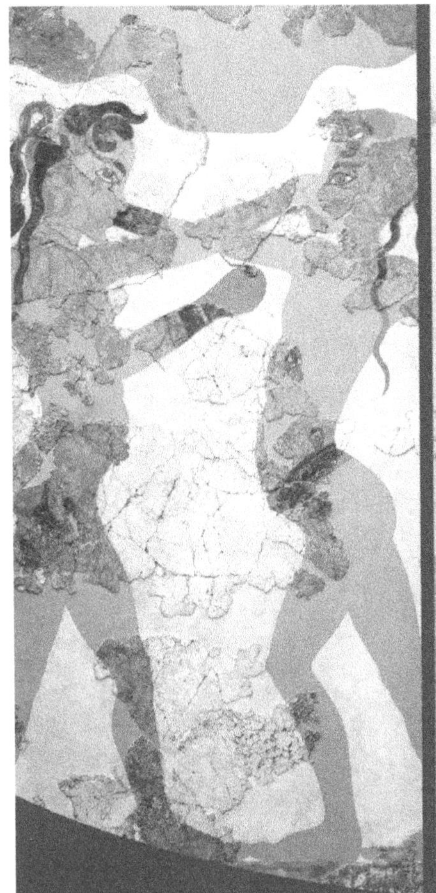

Public domain, via Wikimedia Commons

MINOAN CIVILIZATION

A BRIEF HISTORY FROM BEGINNING TO END

HISTORY HUB

Bonus Downloads

*Get Free Books with **Any Purchase** History Shorts*

Every purchase comes with a FREE download!

Minoan Civilization

A Brief History from Beginning to the End

History Shorts

© 2022 Copyright by History Shorts. All Rights Reserved.

Please Note: The book you are about to enjoy is an analytical review meant for educational and entertainment purposes as an unofficial companion. If you have not yet read the original work, please do before purchasing this copy.

Disclaimer & Terms of Use: No part of this publication may be reproduced or retransmitted, electronic or mechanical, without the written permission of the publisher. The information in this book is meant for educational and entertainment purposes only and the publisher and author make no representations or warranties with respect to the accuracy or completeness of these contents and disclaim all warranties such as warranties of fitness for a particular purpose. Product names, logos, brands, and other trademarks featured or referred to within this publication are the property of their respective trademark holders and are not affiliated with this publication. This is an unofficial summary and analytical review meant for educational and entertainment purposes only and has not been authorized, approved, licensed, or endorsed by the original book's author or publisher and any of their licensees or affiliates.

CONTENTS

Chapter One
Introduction

The Minoan Civilization existed during the Bronze Age on the present-day Island of Crete and other surrounding Aegean Islands. The early beginnings of the Minoans were as early as 3500 BC, but they really came into their own as a successful and culturally advanced society from approximately 2000 BC. They were a very complex and well-developed urban society. From about 1450 BC, their society began to crumble and decline, and by 1100 BC, it had ended. This happened during what is known as the "Greek Dark Ages." During this period, the civilizations of Mycenaean people from late Bronze Age Greece and the Minoans from Crete, and people as far afield as modern Egypt, Turkey, and Israel, collapsed. Cities were abandoned, and writing and art were forgotten. People lived in small pastoral units, and there was mass starvation from famine and drought.

The Minoans were thought to be one of the first advanced civilizations in the world and left behind huge building complexes, wonderfully sophisticated art, and advanced writing systems for archeologists, especially the renowned Sir Arthur Evans, to discover one day.

The Minoan economy boosted trade in the Mediterranean region. It had an enormous impact on other cultures and the growth, development, and spread of Western civilization.

Archeologist Sir Arthur Evans was alerted to the possibility of an ancient Cretan civilization at the beginning of the 20th century when he noted the native Cretans wore ancient seal stones as charms around their necks. When he excavated in 1900 at Knossos, he discovered to his delight, huge and expansive ruins. These confirmed ancient writings of the existence of a sophisticated Cretan culture. Sir Arthur named the civilization Minoan because he believed it could be the site of the labyrinth of King Minos. King Minos was, apparently, an astute man who wrote the Cretan constitution and established naval supremacy, but he was also a cruel tyrant who fed Athenian victims to his Minotaur in his labyrinth. This was to avenge the death of his son. The minotaur was a mythical creature half man and half bull who thrived on human flesh and would hunt young Athenian men who were forced into the Labyrinth of king Minos. Whether King Minos was an actual person or not, the minotaur was definitely a myth, but, as they say, there's no smoke without a fire. There was obviously a great king who had a significant impact on the development and growth of the Minoan Civilization.

The Minoans were seafaring people who were keen traders, and this brought them into contact with many Aegean cultures. This can be seen by the influence of other cultures in their art and pottery and in the materials they used which showed evidence of trade. These included Egyptian ivory and copper from Cyprus.

As with many Ancient Civilizations, there is a fair amount of guesswork and educated deduction from archeologists, which have given us the knowledge and understanding of the Minoan civilization that we will be examining in some detail.

Aegean Contacts

The Minoans, as a seafaring culture, was also in contact with foreign peoples throughout the Aegean, as evidenced by the Near Eastern and Egyptian influences in their early art but also in the later export trade, notably the exchange of pottery and foodstuffs such as oil and wine in return for precious objects and materials such as copper from Cyprus and Attica and ivory from Egypt.

Several other Aegean islands display similar palace-centered economies and the same type of political structure, which was credited to the spread of ideas by the Minoans. There is also ample evidence that Minoan artists, particularly fresco painters, shared their skills in Egypt and Turkey.

Chapter Two
Seafarers or Scribes?

The Minoan Civilization was founded on the Island of Crete and on several islands in the vicinity. These included the island of Thera, which might have caused the demise of Minoan society after a volcanic eruption.

The Minoans were not Greek, but they were closely related, and by trading with the Greeks (Mycenaeans) and other civilizations, including the Egyptians, they soon spread and shared their culture. They sold goods that were extra to their needs and brought back items that they needed for the development of their own economy.

Seafarers

The island of Crete is in the Mediterranean Sea. It has the Aegean Sea on its north shore. It's occasionally called the "stepping stone to the continents" because it's within reach of Asia, Africa, and Europe by boat.

The Mediterranean and the proximity to close trading partners meant that boat-making was an important skill. Minoan ships were about 17 meters long and 3.8 m wide and were built using traditional Bronze Age tools. Trunks from mighty cypress trees were used to form the hulls. They were split and lashed together with plant-based cords, round an A-shaped wooden frame, the tip of which formed the bow. Then the ship was waterproofed with layers of fabric dipped into beef fat and pine resin. The resin was covered with lime and could be decorated with beautiful designs and murals.

Minoan ships were largely made for commerce, but they could be used for war. They took teams of thirty workers about two months to build, and they were rowed by groups of strong, fit men.

Early navigation techniques involved identifying landmarks or following the direction of the sun or stars. Very few bygone sailors sailed out into the open sea. The Minoans were no exception. They would have sailed within view of the land to guide the ship safely. When that was not possible, these ancient sailors observed constellations to mark their place. The ancient Minoans left records of utilizing the stars to navigate.

The navy was almost entirely used for peaceful purposes like trade. There is negligible evidence of any armed conflict in ancient Crete, although having an effective navy could have been preventive and deterrent. Nonetheless, archeology provides no evidence of an army or of Minoans dominating other people like the Mycenaeans. In fact, the opposite is true, as far as we can tell. There is ample evidence of community life, seafaring, religious rituals, and other scenes on the friezes, which give us our main look into the Minoan culture but insignificant evidence that the Minoans were warriors. As always, though, history is open to interpretation, and some experts do see evidence of war scenes on the friezes while others interpret them as religious rituals or blood sports. There is no doubt that the Minoans would have been able to defend themselves if necessary.

Minoan sailors would have been popular as they were skillful and well-trained. There is some evidence that they were vassals of Egyptian royalty and, therefore, that they used their ships in service to the Pharaohs if required. This would probably have been for trade.

Scribes

The Minoans gave birth to at least two different writing systems. The first one was a hieroglyphic-based writing, similar but not identical to the Egyptian hieroglyphic system. This Cretan Hieroglyphic is dated 2000-

1700 BC. One surviving example is the Phaistos Disc. This was found in the ruins of Phaistos, a once-thriving city.

The later style of writing is called Linear A. Linear A is inscribed on clay tablets and is very similar to our style of writing, which moves along lines. We can't be sure if they wrote from right to left or left to right! Unfortunately, to this point in time, no one has succeeded in deciphering the strange Phaistos Disc or the neatly delineated Linear A. Thus, the Minoan language remains a secret, as much as we would love to know what it might reveal.

One other script, called Linear B, was also found on the island of Crete. It was a Mycenean script that was predated by the Minoan script.

Beautifully carved seals that could make impressions in clay, a bit like modern-day signatures, were also a Minoan specialty.

An undeciphered syllabary from Cyprus is called the Cypro-Minoan syllabary and was thought to come from the late Bronze Age. Its similarity to Linear A makes it interesting but still throws little light on the subject. At least 250 objects, including clay balls, votive stands, and tablets containing this elusive writing, have been found.

The Minoans were certainly a diverse and fascinating civilization. Besides being seafarers and scribes, they were also builders, farmers, artists, and crafters.

Chapter Three

Daily Life in Ancient Minoan Civilization

Imagine what it would have been like to live during the Bronze Age. For many early men, this would have meant hunting with a sharpened spear and cutting up the meat with a bronze tool. It would have meant the beginnings of agriculture and better, safer shelters from exposure to the elements. For the Minoans, however, the experience was very sophisticated by comparison.

Minoan Homes

It's quite amazing to believe that the ancient Minoans had many of the amenities of people in our current times, even though they lived more than 4000 years ago.

They lived in big houses with bedrooms and living areas. They had bathrooms that actually had running water. They even had toilets. Although they did not have taps and pipes to carry water, channels brought fresh water and carried away sewerage.

Most contemporary civilizations, if they were settled and not nomads, made their houses from mud bricks, but the Minoans used stone which gave greater protection against exposure to rain and flooding. The Minoans had many luxury items, including gold and silver vessels, gems, and fine jewelry. Other civilizations made and used pottery, but the Minoans decorated their pottery with exquisite, colorful designs, generally with sea themes.

Minoan Food and Medicines

The Minoans were seafaring people who ate fish as their primary protein source. They raised livestock like sheep, cattle, and goats, but they would probably have been used for milk and wool. They did have ritual bull sacrifices occasionally.

The Minoans were farmers as well, and grains like wheat and barley were important to their diet.

In addition to their grain and fish diet, the Minoans cultivated and grew a great variety of fruit, including figs, apples, and pomegranates. The Minoans also grew some grapes which they made into wine and pressed olives to make olive oil which they used for religious ceremonies.

The Minoans also grew a wide variety of herbs which they used for flavoring and curing food and for cosmetics and medicine. They even made some herbs into oils, distilling lavender, mint, sage, and other fragrant herbs to blend for medicine or as perfumes. The priestesses would have undoubtedly enjoyed a fragrant massage from one of the elegant young men who were their acolytes. It's also very likely that the Minoans traded in fine perfumes. They made complex cosmetics using olive oil, beeswax, resin, and honey. They also used the oil of irises. This sought-after substance which was stored in jars elegantly decorated with irises might have been used in funeral rites.

Herbs like anise, coriander, and saffron would have been used for healing purposes and flavoring food. The Minoans had a successful saffron industry.

The Minoans were also keen beekeepers and produced large amounts of honey used for healing, food preparation, and cosmetics. Honey was also used in religious ceremonies.

Minoan Clothing and Fabrics

The Minoans' clothing was typical of the times and suitable for the Mediterranean climate. The men wore loincloths or kilts. The women wore long skirts. These were often paired with a loose open shirt. On cold days, which were rare, both men and women wore wrap-round cloaks. The priestesses wore very revealing skirts which were spilled up to the waist.

The Minoans made much of their clothing from wool, but as they did harvest flax seed, they could make linen too.

Minoan Careers

The Minoans were divided into four social classes. The lower-class people still lived comfortable lives, but they did most of the work. They were farmers, fishermen, traders, and held other useful jobs. There were no slaves, so the common people did all the work. The government was a monarchy that was supported by an efficient bureaucracy. There was no system using money, so goods were traded, and they would be stored at and distributed from the central palaces.

The Minoan priesthood was female, and in fact, many of the entrepreneurs, traders, crafters, and athletes were also women. Women were presumed to be the dominant sex in Minoan society.

Minoan traders traveled by boat and traded in Syria, Egypt, and Asia Minor. They traded olive oil, wine, wool, wood, and olives and secured commodities that they needed to prosper. These would have included copper, tin, silver, gold, emery, precious stones, and ivory.

The Upper-class Minoans, like the upper classes everywhere, had a lot of time to enjoy luxurious lives with lots of good eating, relaxation, and regular spa treatments. Considering the hard lives of other bronze-age cultures, the Minoans lived extremely well. No wonder there has been some speculation about them being the half-god/half-human lost tribe of Atlantis.

Chapter Four
Religion

The Minoan civilization was only rediscovered by the exploration of Sir Arthur Evans in the early 1900s.

Religion - the basics

Details of the Minoan religion remain vague, but certainly interesting elements are uncovered through their art, their architecture, and various significant ritual artifacts. These are largely seen in the friezes showing religious rites and ceremonies, including food offerings, pouring libations, feasts, processions, and sporting events, including the fascinating bull leaping, which was a nonviolent form of bullfighting where an athlete leaped over a charging bull. Nature, in general, seemed to be worshiped or at least highly admired. The earth mother goddess figures were often depicted surrounded by animals.

Palatial mansions included open courtyards, which were used for mass gatherings, like religious ceremonies, and certain rooms had wells and open drainage channels into which to pour libations. Bulls appeared as prominent symbols and probably had religious significance.

The Gods and Goddesses.

Mother Goddess

Academics think that the primary Minoan deity was a goddess, perhaps one of the mother goddess figures, that dominated many ancient cultures. She was frequently attended by a young male, which scholars speculate could be a son, lover, or religious devotee. Some intellectuals think that she could have been a solar deity. The Minoan deity is frequently shown with various animals or mythical beasts and creatures and is believed to have been adored as a sole deity with different characteristics. She appears in the iconography of the friezes as a goddess of mountains, doves, snakes, poppies, animals, and childbirth.

Many terracotta statuettes have been uncovered from Cretan archaeological sites and have been dated to the pre-Minoan Neolithic period. These are typical ancient earth mother goddess figurines, large-breasted and wide-hipped women squatting as if to give birth. They had no feet and small heads. Intellectuals have linked them to fertility and childbirth. They were probably utilized to bless homes or to ease delivery. Interestingly though, during the main period of Minoan civilization, figures appeared showing women in ceremonial dress. These sculptures were initially thought to depict the Minoan snake goddess. Still, various scholars now think that they were more likely to be representations of a priestess or even of a priestess queen Archeology indicates a move away from the earth-motherly aspects of the female goddess during this period which is known as neo palatial. They indicate that this was superseded by a religious following devoted to the young male god, who was thought to be both son and lover of the goddess.

In 1903, two female statuettes holding snakes were dug up from the site of the palace at Knossos. These were thought to symbolize creation, life, and wisdom.

These statuettes revealed women in intricate clothing, although bare-breasted, with a snake in each of their hands. Though Sir Arthur Evans, who found these items, believed one to depict a snake priestess and the other to depict a snake goddess, there has been no peer-reviewed agreement on whether these idols were goddesses or priestesses. Snake images are found in many additional religions, including Aboriginal mythology, Christianity, Incan theology, and Greek paganism. The snake was extremely significant in Greek pagan theology, where it depicted healing magic, prophecy, and spiritual power. It may be that the Minoans did not, in fact, honor a snake goddess. There is limited evidence besides these idols. The snakes might have depicted the prophetic or spiritual power of the priestess.

The Minoan deity seems to have been attended to by a devout sect of priestesses. Academics have implied that these priestesses may have emulated the goddess during ceremonies. If this is the case, it is hard to differentiate between portrayals of rulers, deities, priestesses, and priests in Minoan sculptures and iconography. Some scholars have indicated that the positions of monarch and priest may have been combined in Minoan civilization, with leading religious rituals seen as a crucial role of political leadership. Some academics think that characterizations of the Minoan goddess demonstrate that Minoan society was intrinsically matriarchal, but others assert that the portrayals show priestesses, not a goddess, and therefore cannot be indicated as evidence of a matriarchal society or of the political superiority of Minoan women.

Other Deities

Pictures have been uncovered of the Minoan goddess represented as a dove. Archeologists found various vases and charms shaped like birds dating to the Early Minoan era. They also discovered clay figurines of doves in the palace at Knossos, especially at the religious shrines. Academics believe these doves were used for ceremonies. Additionally, many late Minoan terracotta votive sculptures of the goddess exhibit her attended by birds.

Chapter Five

Cities and Buildings

Crete is a beautiful mountainous island that has many natural harbors. It's a volatile area with clear signs of damage caused by earthquakes at many ancient Minoan sites. There are also obvious signs of land disturbance and the submersion of shoreline sites because of earthquake damage along the coast.

Homer mentioned that Crete had ninety cities. Based on the sites of palaces, the island was presumably divided into approximately eight political divisions at the pinnacle of the Minoan civilization. Most Minoan districts are in eastern and central Crete, with some in the west.

There seem to have been four main ruling palaces on Crete. These were Phaistos, Knossos, Kato Zakros, and Malia, and each ruled a major section of Crete, although there were smaller palaces as well.

Major settlements

Knossos was thought to be the biggest Bronze Age archaeological site evident on Crete. Knossos had an approximate population of 100,000 in

1600 BC, which was during its prime, but that had dropped to 30,000 by 1360 BC.

Phaistos was the second-largest palace building in Crete. It was uncovered by the Italian archaeological school shortly after Sir Arthur Evans excavated Knossos.

Malia was the task of French archeologists. It was a palatial center that furnished a glimpse into the advanced proto-palatial period.

Kato Zakros was a seaside palatial location excavated by a group of Greek archaeologists.

Other less significant sites were Galatas, Kydonia, Hagia Kydonia, the home of Linear A tablets, Giurnia, Pyrgos, Vasikili, Fournou Korfi, Pseira, Mount Juktas, Akrotiri, Karfi and Zominthos.

Buildings

At each one of these archaeological sites, there is evidence of huge, intricate palace structures that seem to have functioned as local trade, administrative, religious, and political centers. Unfortunately, the connection between the palatial buildings and the government structure is not obvious, owing to insufficient archaeological and scholarly evidence. It is apparent, however, that the palaces wielded some sort of localized control. This was particularly in the collecting and warehousing of excess materials like oil, wine, cereals, gold and bronze, and pottery. Little villages and farms circled the territory apparently governed by each of these palaces. Roads joined these solitary settlements to one another and to the main center. There is a widespread agreement among historiographers that the palaces were autonomous until 1700 BC, and subsequently, they were governed by Knossos.

The scarcity of fortresses in the settlements indicates a fairly benign co-existence between the various population groups. The roads, however, had evidence of regularly placed watchtowers indicating that bandits might have plagued unprotected travelers.

The palaces were beautifully designed with enormous structures with huge courtyards and colonnades. The ceilings were supported by wooden columns, and there were lofty staircases, sacred crypts, substantial drainage systems, vast storage areas, and even 'theater' rooms for public shows or religious ceremonies.

These buildings reached up to four stories in height and covered many thousands of square meters. These huge labyrinthian palaces, decorated by bull horns, probably gave rise to the story of Theseus and the formidable Minotaur.

Chapter Six
Art

The Minoans were ahead of their time in both their artistic creations and their use of writing.

Art

An illustration of a civilization's elevated degree of evolution is the variation and excellence of its art forms. The art forms practiced by the Minoan civilization were very advanced. Finds of pottery uncovered a vast range of containers and other vessels, from delicate cups to large utilitarian storage jars which are called pithoi. Ceramic items were originally hand-turned, but after 1700 BC were made on a potter's wheel, which is a significant technological advance. In adornment and trimming, there was an interesting advancement from the earlier flowing, elegant geometric designs in Kamares ware to bright, lifelike images of plants, flowers, sea creatures, and waves in the later Marine and Floral styles. Popular pottery shapes included items like amphorae with three handles, beaked jugs for milk or water, strange spherical vessels with false spouts, a variety of beakers, small boxes with attractive lids, and a range of ceremonial vessels with handles shaped like figures of eight. Stone was as popular as clay and was used to create similar vessels which would have been hardier. Stone was also used to produce rhyta which were ritual containers used for sprinkling libations. These were often shaped like animal heads.

Large sculptures did not survive, but many figurines were found in the archaeological digs made from bronze and other precious materials. Clay sculptures showed the clothing of that age, with men dressed in loincloths and women wearing long elegant skirts and jackets which opened in the front.

The Minoans were well known for their majestic frescoes, which were carved and painted on the ceilings, walls, and floors of their grand palaces. These frescoes also used nature and sea themes. They reveal details about their community, religious and funeral practices. The frescoes showed subjects on a scale from miniature to bigger than life. The Minoans liked to paint scenes without humans in them, representing their love of nature. They painted birds, animals like monkeys, and sea creatures like dolphins in their natural habitat. Often the scenes from the fresco's covered many walls.

The Minoans are known for their labyrinthian palaces, and beautiful frescoes illustrating scenes such as bull-leaping and religious processions. They made delicate gold jewelry, as well as beautiful stone vases and earthenware with rich symbols of marine life and botany.

The Voice of Art

Minoan art tells us a lot about their culture. The Minoan religion appeared to have a goddess at its center. The goddess is commonly depicted as carrying two snakes.

The bull also had an important role in Minoan culture. Bulls were brought to Crete by people, and they had religious significance. The Minoan palaces have numerous carvings of bull horns.

Frescoes also demonstrated that men and women went to meetings and functions together, implying that women and men shared the same social status. The frescoes also indicate to us that the Minoans appreciated spectator sports, particularly that very energetic sport, bull leaping.

Minoan art was not only a real joy to see and enjoy, and it had real uses as well.

Are You Enjoying Reading?

As an independent publisher

with a tiny marketing budget

we rely on readers, like you.

If you're receiving help from this book,

would you please take a moment to write a brief review?

We really appreciate it.

Chapter Seven
Minoan Myths

The Minoan Civilization was named by Sir Arthur Evans after the mythological king Minos.

The Minotaur

The Minotaur, which comes from the word Minotauras (Minos's Bull), was a terrible animal with the body of a man and the head of a bull. The Minotaur was the offspring of Pasiphae, who was the wife of Minos, and a beautiful snow-white bull that had been sent to Minos by the sea god Poseidon to sacrifice. Minos ignored the injunction of the god and kept the bull.

An enraged Poseidon made Pasiphae fall in love with the bull, and in a bizarre mating ritual involving a mechanical cow, Pasiphae was impregnated. The child, a hideous monster, was incarcerated in a Labyrinth that was made by Daedalus for Minos.

When the son of Minos, Androgens, was killed by Athenians, Minos was enraged and demanded an annual sacrifice of seven Athenian men and seven Athenian maidens to be eaten by the Minotaur. The Athenian hero, Theseus, insisted on joining the group to be sacrificed and, with the aid of Minos's daughter Ariadne killed the Minotaur, and then they ran away together.

Minos was killed by the daughters of King Cocalus, who poured boiling water over him. He then became a judge in Hades.

In reality, however, and despite Athenian grievances, Minos was a just and powerful ruler. In fact, the name Minos might apply a dynastic or royal title to the kinds of Minoans.

Britomartis

Britomartis was thought to be the goddess of hunters, fishermen, and mountains for the Minoan civilization that developed on the Crete between 2700 to 1450 BC. There are numerous incompatible aspects of the Britomartis tale in Greek mythology. This is probably due to it having arisen from an earlier culture before evolving and adapting to changing Greek ideas as their civilization grew in impact and strength.

Britomartis was born to Zeus and Carme and on Crete as a Cretan nymph. She came to be a huntress and killed the wild creatures in the

Cretan forests. She was a friend of Artemis, becoming strongly associated with her, as they both shared a desire to remain virgins.

When Minos, king of Crete, saw Britomartis, he instantly fell in love. Minos was also a son of Zeus, although Europa was his mother, and so he was her half-brother. Such a marriage would have been distasteful to her, although it did not bother him.

Britomartis was not at all enamored with Minos, who tried to rape her. She fled and evaded him. She was a quick, powerful runner, but she could not shake him off, and the hunt was proclaimed to have lasted for nine long months before he finally succeeded in trapping her on the edge of a cliff over the sea.

Although caught, Britomartis tossed herself from the cliff into the sea. She would rather die than relinquish her virginity to Minos. Fortunately, she was saved by passing fishermen who saved her in their nets

Her pal Artemis was extremely impressed by her decision to keep her innocence intact and made her goddess of hunters, shores, mountains, fishermen, ports, and nets.

Chapter Eight
Why Minoan Civilization Declined

There has been ongoing historical debate about the fall of the Minoans. People want to understand why the virtual gods of the ancient world should have fallen so dramatically.

Fire and Fury

Possible explanations for the death of the Minoan civilization continue to be punted among academics. There's no doubt that in 1450 BC, many of the settlements and palaces showed significant evidence of fire damage except at Knossos, which was destroyed about a hundred years later.

It seems likely, according to the writings of Greek archeologist Spyridon Marinatos that the eruption of the island of Thera, which is present-day Santorini, between 1550 and 1500 BC, caused ash fallout and tsunamis which could have fatally damaged much of Minoan culture. The volcano was thought to have ejected between 60 and 100 cubic kilometers of fire, lava, rock, ash, and dust into the atmosphere.

The Minoan settlement on Santorini was buried in a thick layer of pumice, and a huge Tsunami flooded a large part of coastal Crete. Original theories suggested that the ash choked the plant life, which subsequently caused the population to starve, but later fieldwork indicated that the ash layer was not thick enough to have caused the catastrophic environmental demise.

So, what did cause the end of Minoan Civilization? Was it fire and brimstone, or did the ancient Minoans limp into oblivion?

Limping into Oblivion

There are enough remains above the Thera ash layer to imply that the eruption and the Tsunami did not, in fact, wipe out Minoan culture completely in an Atlantis-like event. The Minoans were a seafaring nation, though, and the loss of ships and harbors could have caused enough financial hardship and political and economic weakness to make them vulnerable to attack by other powers, probably the Mycenaeans. There was a substantial influence of Mycenaean art, architecture, and culture on Crete from this time. The Thera eruption might have signified the beginning of the end of Minoan glory. It's probable, looking at archeological evidence, which indicated that much of the Minoan empire was destroyed by fire, that this was fire from invasion rather than from a natural disaster because Knossos was not badly damaged at first which suggests that an invading force saw the value of preserving the buildings of the city. There is also environmental evidence that the Minoans exceeded the carrying capacity of their island through significant deforestation, which would have limited their ability to recover.

The likeliest scenario was probably a combination of severe environmental damage and competition to make a living in a fractured society. This would have made them vulnerable to the invasion of the Mycenaeans, which would have meant the dilution of the Minoan culture.

Whether their downfall was caused quickly or slowly, it was impacted by the Thera eruption, and the like of Minoans were not seen again in the past world for hundreds of years. Crete stood abandoned until the 8th century when the Archaic Greeks colonized it again.

Chapter Nine

Were the Minoans from Atlantis?

The Minoans had a significant effect on history. They developed the world's first settled civilization, and they shared it with other nations. One interesting philosophy is that the sophisticated lost world described by Plato could actually have been the Minoans.

The Minoans were an advanced civilization.

Although most of Europe was inhabited by small nomadic tribes, the Minoans developed a sophisticated economic and political system that has had an impact on history right up to modern times. They appeared almost as if dropped by the gods and filled their space and that of their neighbors and other countries with technology, art, and culture. They proved to be extremely innovative.

The Minoans were inventive and prepared to learn from cultures. They took what they learned from Egypt, Mesopotamia, and Persia and improved upon their technologies. Their architecture was extremely advanced and stylish.

Minoan palaces showed unprecedented skills for that time. One can see where the legend of the Labyrinth came from. A culture as sophisticated as that of the Minoans might well have been able to establish an impenetrable fortress as the Labyrinth described in mythology. The Minoans cleverly combined materials to create their magnificent buildings. They even left rubble at the base of the foundations and walls, ostensibly to absorb seismic shock and make them less vulnerable to earthquakes which were common in that area.

The Minoans also created sophisticated water systems using wells, cisterns, underground pipes, and even aqueducts. There was evidence of a culture of bathing, which was unusual at that time.

The Minoans were skilled crafters, enjoying working with stone, but they also learned the art of delicate pottery with the arrival of the potter's wheel somewhere between 1900 and 1700 BC. They also carved the seal stones, which alerted Sir Arthur Evans to a sophisticated culture lost beneath the sands. These carved gemstone seal stones could be used to "sign" wax or clay tablets.

Atlantis?

Some Scientists and historians believe that the Atlantis that Plato spoke of was a real civilization and that it might have been the home of the Minoan culture, which seemed to rise dramatically and unexpectedly.

At the height of their strange and unexpected power, the Minoans suddenly disappeared. Plato described the lost world of Atlantis, which had disappeared under the sea, as a great and sophisticated culture of half men and half gods. Whether Plato researched this story as he claimed from ancient Egyptian manuscripts or whether it was a great story, one can never know, but it's believed that in 1600 BC, a great earthquake caused the volcanic island of Thera to erupt, sending millions of tons of volcanic ash and rock into the atmosphere. Tsunamis were caused, which could well have damaged the sophisticated culture of the Minoans, leaving them impoverished and vulnerable to attack, or maybe it could have sunk their culture under the waves forever, as Plato suggested. It's another of the theories around the fall of the Minoan civilization, and while it's largely discredited, it still has a nice ring to it.

Chapter Ten
The Modern Minoans

Historians have long believed that the Minoans were part of a strange sophisticated culture or from the lost world of Atlantis or even from out of space.

Modern DNA studies, however, have shown that the Minoans were very close to their backyard.

The modern Greeks, according to studies of ancient DNA, are the descendants of the Minoans of Crete and the Mycenaeans of modern-day mainland Greece.

The Minoans and the Mycenaeans were the direct ancestors of those who lived in classical Greece some thousand years later. They were populations that arose no further than Western Anatolia (Part of Turkey) and Greece.

The Minoan and Mycenaean cultures had a significant impact on Greek and European society. This first real civilization built sophisticated buildings, created beautiful art, and even had its own written language, which, although never deciphered, seems similar in form to ancient Greek. The Linear A and later developed Linear B scripts seem to have defined similarities to ancient Greek writings, although nothing is definite about the origins of an extinct language that is part of a vanished civilization, even if there are some similarities.

In fact, until quite recently, it was believed that the Minoans came from a more advanced society in another location somewhere and that when they had established their culture, they shared it during trade and exploration with the Mycenaeans of the Greek mainland

Johannes Krause of the Max Planck Institute for the Science of Human History decided to do some DNA research on the subject. His reasoning was as follows, "We wanted to determine if the people who made up the Minoan and Mycenaean populations were actually genetically distinct or not. How were they related to each other? Who were their ancestors? And how are modern Greeks related to them?"

The group of researchers studied genomes from nineteen individuals. These included Minoans, Mycenaeans, an individual from the Greek mainland, and some bronze age specimens from Western Anatolia. This was no mean task, as the preservation of DNA is notoriously poor in the damp heat of the Mediterranean climate.

This archaeogenetics study was a collaboration between researchers at Harvard and researchers at Washington University in Seattle and was published in the top scientific journal Nature.

The research found conclusively that the Minoans and Mycenaeans were closely genetically related, although differences did exist. They seemed to have a common ancestor, which they shared with Bronze Age Anatolians. This ancestor was from a Neolithic Anatolian grouping and other groups of people related to populations in Iran and in the Caucasus.

This was interesting because it was originally thought that the eastern ancestors originated from Steppe pastoralists, but the Minoans did not share the genes of the northern steppe nomadic pastoralists even though mainland Greeks did.

What is definite is the modern Greeks have close genetic ties to Mycenaeans and Minoans. The Greeks were described as a "work in progress," according to Iosif Lazaridis of the Harvard Medical School, who was one of the main authors of the genetic study. They had considerable input from migrations across the ages, but it is interesting to note that

even from the Minoan times, much of their genetics were homegrown.

Chapter Eleven
Conclusion

Lessons from History

The Minoan civilization rose, and it fell again into obscurity, its people decimated, and its skills, art, and culture lost. Can the fall of civilizations teach us how to stop the likely fall of our own?

The size and the sophistication of civilization, as the Minoans taught us, are not necessarily a barrier to collapse and failure. The Mayans, the Phoenicians, the Romans, the Mongolians, and many others have risen, made their mark, and disappeared

Modern civilization, despite its globalization and its technical advances, is not immune to sinking into obscurity either.

A study by Dr. Luke Kemp points out that there are enough common traits between ancient and modern civilizations to indicate that modern society could end up in the same situation as collapsed civilizations. Dire situations like climate change could well end our lucky streak on this planet if we do not learn from the lessons of history

Dr. Kemp reminds us, "We haven't actually outlasted the average of most species yet," but "if we can take the right lessons of the past, they can be a very safe guide to the future."

So what can we do using the lessons from History to protect our future? People talk about a "collapsed civilization." This is where the stresses placed on civilization are big enough to destroy the coping mechanisms of that society.

This could happen abruptly, as it probably did in the case of the Minoans, who were left so damaged by natural disasters that they could not rebuild their civilization and succumbed to external threats, or it could happen as it is in our modern civilization, death by pinpricks.

Sometimes this collapse could be beneficial. The collapse of Mesopotamia, where 1 in 3 people were slaves, meant the beginnings of a better society. The collapse of modern civilization could save the planet or, even better, prompt people to save the earth before civilization collapses. The collapse of civilizations could prompt a factory reset. People would have to rethink what's important to them.

Periods after a collapse can bring rejuvenation, whereas more complex societies with sophisticated weaponry and an economy that demands them to become the "head of the pack" and their resulting greed could cause a nightmarishly severe collapse, like a nuclear war.

If people examine the lessons of history, they could avoid disaster and create a better space for all. We should take the lessons of collapsed civilizations like the Minoans on board

Chapter Twelve
Discussion Question

The Minoan civilization collapsed by 1100 BC. This was followed by a period called the Greek Dark Ages. What does this mean? What caused it?

Discussion Question

The Minoans were a matriarchal society. Is this true? What evidence do you have for this? And against?

Discussion Question

The Minoans were keen sailors. How did they build their boats? Did being a seafaring nation assist with their growth and civilization?

Discussion Question

The religion of the Minoans was quite confusing. Explain the roles of the goddess and priestesses to show how the confusion arose. What's your opinion?

Discussion Question

Minoan art was fascinating. What do the designs tell you about their culture? What materials were popular for their creation?

Discussion Question

Minoan friezes to stories. What type of stories did they tell? How was

their civilization advanced?

Discussion Question

Minoans fascinated archeologists. Why do you think this is? Which other civilizations would you have enjoyed exploring?

Discussion Question

What did Minoans do to earn a living? List and discuss three career

options. Which do you think would have interested you?

Chapter Thirteen

Quiz Question

1. **True/False:** The Minoan goddess was represented as an earth mother. She was short and fat. She squatted in the delivery position.

2. **True/False:** Minoans had one type of writing. It was a similar hieroglyphic system to the Egyptians. It was simpler, though.

3. **True/False:** The Minoans built war machines and fortified cities. They were fierce warriors. They threw their enemies into the sea.

4. **True/False:** The Minoans had excess olive oil. They used it to trade. It was popular among the people of that time for religious ceremonies.

5. **True/ False:** The Minoans had a king called Minos. That name might have referred to the royal dynasty, though. He was a mythical king.

6. **True/False:** The Minoans played a dangerous sport called bull baiting, where they tortured a bull. They often were injured. It was very cruel.

7. **True/False:** The Minoans were believed, by some scholars, to be from the lost city of Atlantis. This seemed unlikely to other scholars, though. No one can be sure..

8. **True/ False:** The Minoans navigated their boats by staying close to
land. They also used the sun. Records show that they also navigated by
looking at the stars.

Quiz Answer

1. False: The Minoan goddess was represented as tall and elegant. She was attended by a young male god or acolyte.

2. False: The Minoans had at least two types of writing. The second one was linear like ours.

3. False: The Minoans appeared to have been peaceful people.

4. True

5. True.

6. False: They played a sport called bull leaping, a test of agility that did not injure an animal.

7. True

8. True

Bibliography

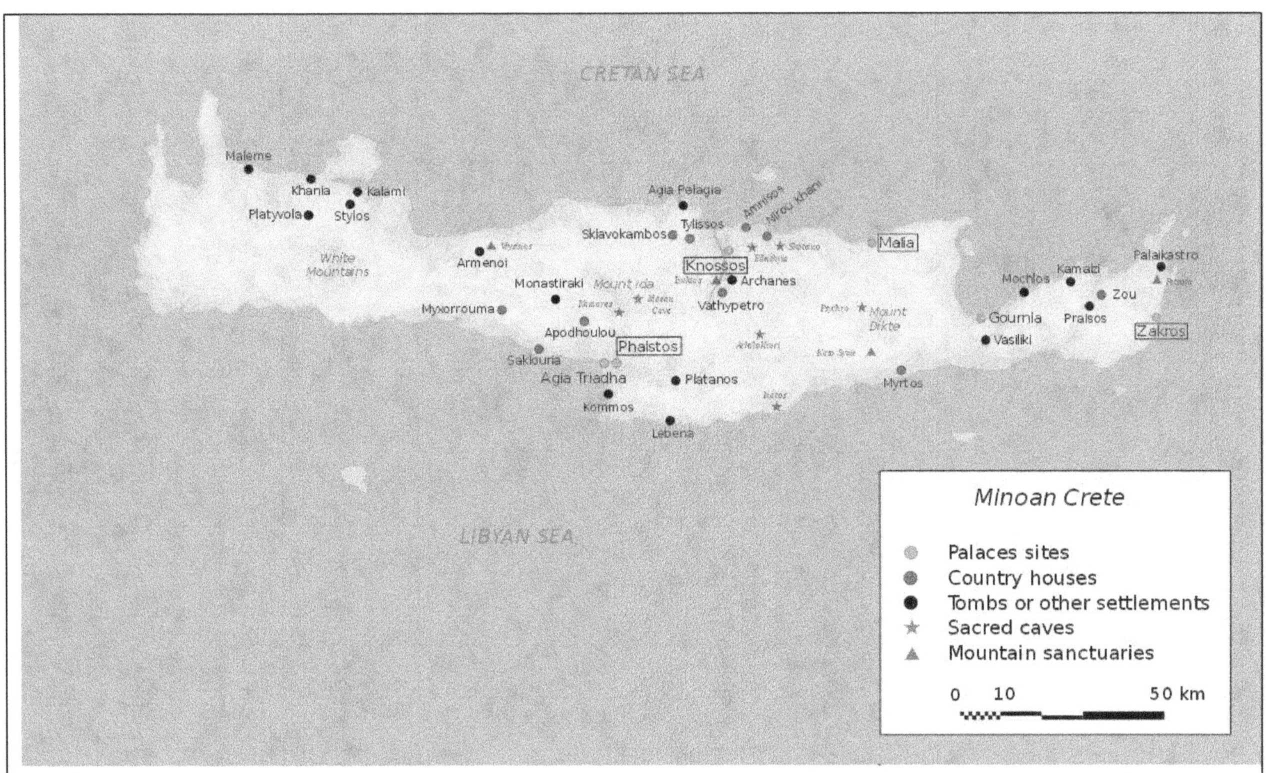

Opening

The Minoan Civilization existed during the Bronze Age on the present-day Island of Crete and other surrounding Aegean Islands. The early beginnings of the Minoans were as early as 3500 BC, but they really came into their own as a successful and culturally advanced society from approximately 2000 BC. They were a very complex and well-developed urban society Wikipedia

The Palace of Knossos

Most contemporary civilizations, if they were settled and not nomads, made their houses from mud bricks, but the Minoans used stone which gave greater protection against exposure to rain and flooding. The Minoans had many luxury items, including gold and silver vessels, gems, and fine jewelry. Other civilizations made and used pottery, but the Minoans decorated their pottery with exquisite, colorful designs, generally with sea themes. (Wikipedia)

Minoan Fashion

The Minoans' clothing was typical of the times and suitable for the Mediterranean climate. The men wore loincloths or kilts. The women wore long skirts. These were often paired with a loose open shirt. On cold days, which were rare, both men and women wore wrap-round cloaks. The priestesses wore very revealing skirts which were spilled up to the waist.

(Wikipedia)

Sewers of the Palace of Knossos

The Minoans were thought to be one of the first advanced civilizations in the world. They left behind huge building complexes, wonderfully sophisticated art, and advanced writing systems for archeologists, especially the renowned Sir Arthur Evans, to discover one day (Wikipedia)

The Minotaur

The Minotaur, which comes from the word Minotauras (Minos's Bull), was a terrible animal with the body of a man and the head of a bull. The Minotaur was the offspring of Pasiphae, who was the wife of Minos, and a beautiful snow-white bull that had been sent to Minos by the sea god Poseidon to sacrifice. Minos ignored the injunction of the god and kept the bull. (Wikipedia)

Atlantis?

Some Scientists and historians believe that the Atlantis that Plato spoke of was a real civilization and that it might have been the home of the Minoan culture, which seemed to rise dramatically and unexpectedly.

At the height of their strange and unexpected power, the Minoans suddenly disappeared. Plato described the lost world of Atlantis, which had disappeared under the sea, as a great and sophisticated culture of half men and half gods.

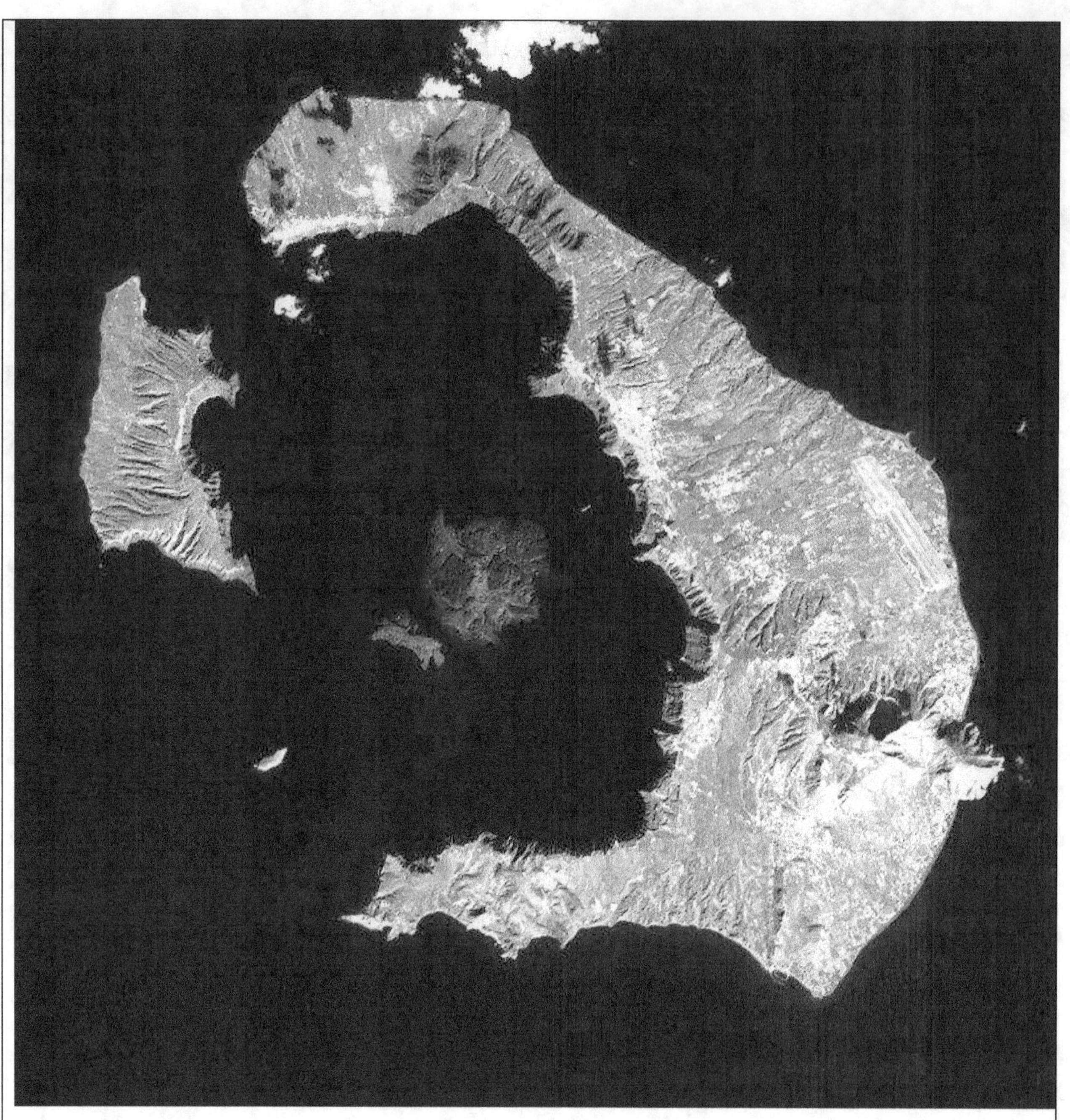

Closing

The Thera eruption might have signified the beginning of the end of

Minoan glory. It's probable, looking at archeological evidence, which

indicated that much of the Minoan empire was destroyed by fire, that this was fire from invasion rather than from a natural disaster because Knossos was not badly damaged at first which suggests that an invading force saw the value of preserving the buildings of the city. There is also environmental evidence that the Minoans exceeded the carrying capacity of their island through significant deforestation, which would have limited their ability to recover.

(Wikipedia)

Bonus Downloads

*Get Free Books with **<u>Any Purchase</u>** History Shorts*

Every purchase comes with a FREE download!

Thank You For Reading

As an independent publisher

with a tiny marketing budget

we rely on readers, like you.

If you're receiving help from this book,

would you please take a moment to write a brief review?

We really appreciate it.

www.ingramcontent.com/pod-product-compliance
Lightning Source LLC
Chambersburg PA
CBHW081314150726
48001CB00022B/3113

* 9 7 9 8 2 2 3 6 8 9 8 9 8 *